19.95

The NFL's Greatest Teams

Washington Redskins

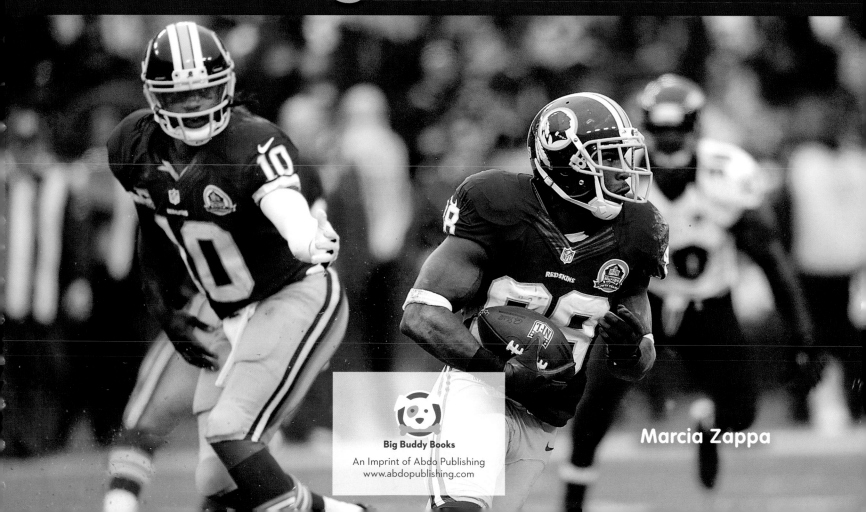

Marcia Zappa

Big Buddy Books
An Imprint of Abdo Publishing
www.abdopublishing.com

www.abdopublishing.com

Published by Abdo Publishing, a division of ABDO, PO Box 398166, Minneapolis, Minnesota 55439.
Copyright © 2015 by Abdo Consulting Group, Inc. International copyrights reserved in all countries. No part
of this book may be reproduced in any form without written permission from the publisher. Big Buddy Books™
is a trademark and logo of Abdo Publishing.

Printed in the United States of America, North Mankato, Minnesota.
092014
012015

Cover Photo: ASSOCIATED PRESS.
Interior Photos: ASSOCIATED PRESS (pp. 5, 7, 9, 11, 13, 15, 17, 18, 19, 20, 21, 23, 25, 27, 28, 29); MCT via
    Getty Images (p. 22).

Coordinating Series Editor: Rochelle Baltzer
Contributing Editors: Bridget O'Brien, Sarah Tieck
Graphic Design: Michelle Labatt

Library of Congress Cataloging-in-Publication Data

Zappa, Marcia, 1985-
  Washington Redskins / Marcia Zappa.
     pages cm. -- (The NFL's Greatest Teams)
  Audience: Age: 7-11.
  ISBN 978-1-62403-592-0
  1. Washington Redskins (Football team)--History--Juvenile literature. I. Title.
  GV956.W3Z37 2015
  796.332'6409753--dc23
                       2014026422

Contents

A Winning Team

The Washington Redskins are a football team based in Washington DC. They have played in the National Football League (NFL) for more than 80 years.

The Redskins have had good seasons and bad. But time and again, they've proven themselves. Let's see what makes the Redskins one of the NFL's greatest teams.

Burgundy and gold are the team's colors.

League Play

The NFL got its start in 1920. Its teams have changed over the years. Today, there are 32 teams. They make up two conferences and eight divisions.

The Redskins play in the East Division of the National Football Conference (NFC). This division also includes the Dallas Cowboys, the New York Giants, and the Philadelphia Eagles.

Team Standings

The NFC and the American Football Conference (AFC) make up the NFL. Each conference has a north, south, east, and west division.

The Cowboys are a major rival of the Redskins.

7

Kicking Off

The Redskins were founded in 1932 by George Preston Marshall. At first, the team was based in Boston, Massachusetts. They were called the Boston Braves.

In 1933, the team's name changed to the Boston Redskins. In 1937, Marshall moved the Redskins to Washington DC.

The Redskins had their first winning season in 1936. They continued to succeed in the following years.

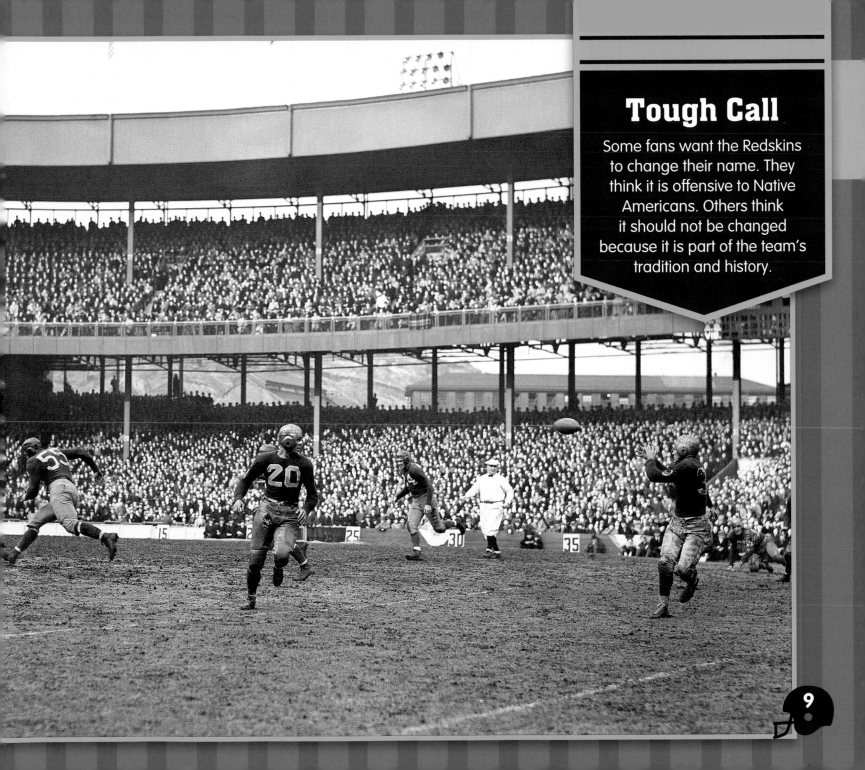

Tough Call

Some fans want the Redskins to change their name. They think it is offensive to Native Americans. Others think it should not be changed because it is part of the team's tradition and history.

Highlight Reel

The Redskins did well in their new city. In 1937, they **drafted** star quarterback Sammy Baugh. He helped them become NFL **champions** his first year! In 1942, Baugh led the team to a second championship win.

Then, the team struggled for many years. In 1971, George Allen became head coach. He helped the Redskins make the play-offs his first year. In 1973, the team played in its first Super Bowl. But, they lost.

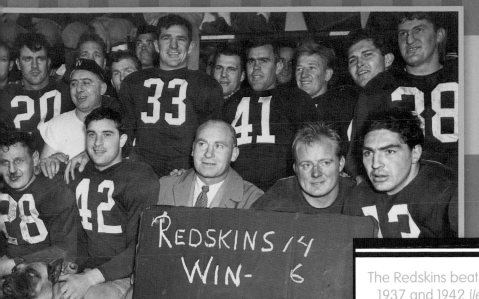

The Redskins beat the Chicago Bears in the 1937 and 1942 (*left*) NFL championships.

In the 1973 Super Bowl, the Redskins lost to the undefeated Miami Dolphins 14–7.

11

In 1981, Joe Gibbs became head coach. He led the team to success. The Redskins made it to the Super Bowl in 1983, 1984, 1988, and 1992. They won in 1983, 1988, and 1992!

Starting in the mid-1990s, the Redskins struggled again. In 2012, they **drafted** quarterback Robert Griffin III. He led them to many wins his first season. Today, the Redskins are trying to get back to their former glory.

Win or Go Home

NFL teams play 16 regular season games each year. The teams with the best records are part of the play-off games. Play-off winners move on to the conference championships. Then, conference winners face off in the Super Bowl!

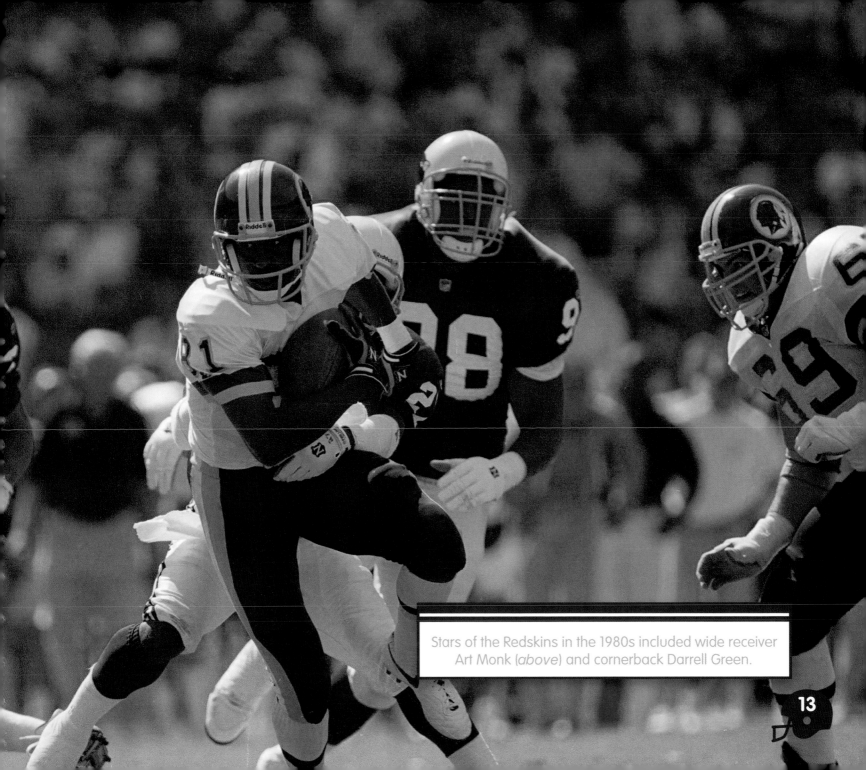

Stars of the Redskins in the 1980s included wide receiver Art Monk (*above*) and cornerback Darrell Green.

Halftime! Stat Break

Team Records

RUSHING YARDS
Career: John Riggins, 7,472 yards (1976–1979, 1981–1985)
Single Season: Alfred Morris, 1,613 yards (2012)
PASSING YARDS
Career: Joe Theismann, 25,206 yards (1974–1985)
Single Season: Jay Schroeder, 4,109 yards (1986)
RECEPTIONS
Career: Art Monk, 888 receptions (1980–1993)
Single Season: Pierre Garcon, 113 receptions (2013)
ALL-TIME LEADING SCORER
Mark Moseley, 1,206 points, (1974–1986)

Fan Fun

NICKNAMES: The Burgundy and Gold
STADIUM: FedExField
LOCATION: Landover, Maryland
TEAM SONG: "Hail to the Redskins"

Championships

EARLY CHAMPIONSHIP WINS:
1937, 1942

SUPER BOWL APPEARANCES:
1973, 1983, 1984, 1988, 1992

SUPER BOWL WINS:
1983, 1988, 1992

Famous Coaches

George Allen (1971–1977)
Joe Gibbs (1981–1992, 2004–2007)

Pro Football Hall of Famers & Their Years with the Redskins

George Allen, Coach (1971–1977)
Cliff Battles, Halfback (1932–1937)
Sammy Baugh, Quarterback (1937–1952)
Bill Dudley, Halfback (1950–1951, 1953)
Albert Glen (Turk) Edwards, Tackle (1932–1940)
Ray Flaherty, Coach (1936–1942)
Joe Gibbs, Coach (1981–1992, 2004–2007)
Darrell Green, Cornerback (1983–2002)
Russ Grimm, Guard (1981–1991)
Chris Hanburger, Linebacker (1965–1978)
Ken Houston, Strong Safety (1973–1980)
Sam Huff, Linebacker (1964–1967, 1969)
Sonny Jurgensen, Quarterback (1964–1974)
George Preston Marshall, Founder-Owner (1932–1969)
Wayne Millner, End (1936–1941, 1945)
Bobby Mitchell, Wide Receiver/Halfback (1962–1968)
Art Monk, Wide Receiver (1980–1993)
John Riggins, Running Back (1976–1979, 1981–1985)
Charley Taylor, Wide Receiver (1964–1975, 1977)

Coaches' Corner

In 1971, George Allen took over a struggling Redskins team. He made many trades for skilled players. Soon, the team started winning. In just his second season as head coach, Allen led the Redskins to their first Super Bowl.

Joe Gibbs became head coach in 1981. He led the Redskins for 12 seasons. During that time, the team had only one losing season. With Gibbs, they made it to the Super Bowl four times and won three times.

The Redskins had no losing seasons during Allen's seven seasons as head coach.

Jay Gruden became head coach in 2014.

After his success in the 1980s and 1990s, Gibbs returned as coach from 2004 to 2007. But, the team wasn't able to repeat its championship play.

Star Players

Sammy Baugh QUARTERBACK (1937–1952)

Sammy Baugh was the team's first pick in the 1937 draft. He was a quarterback and a punter. He also played defense. In 1943, Baugh led the NFL in passing, punting, and interceptions. He helped change the NFL by making pass plays more popular.

Sonny Jurgensen QUARTERBACK (1964–1974)

Sonny Jurgensen played for the team for 11 seasons. He was known for his **accurate** passing. During his time with the Redskins, Jurgensen led the NFL in passing three seasons. He helped the Redskins make it to their first Super Bowl.

Chris Hanburger LINEBACKER (1965–1978)

Chris Hanburger was chosen late in the 1965 **draft**. Soon, he became a leader on the team's defense. Hanburger helped the Redskins make it to their first Super Bowl. And, he played in the Pro Bowl, which is the NFL's all-star game, eight times.

Joe Theismann QUARTERBACK (1974–1985)

Joe Theismann played for the Redskins his whole NFL career. He led them to two Super Bowls and helped them win one. In 1983, he was named the NFL's Most Valuable Player (MVP). By the time he retired, he had thrown for 25,206 yards. That is more than any other Redskin.

Art Monk WIDE RECEIVER (1980–1993)

Art Monk was the team's first pick in the 1980 draft. That year, Monk had 58 receptions. That set a team record for a rookie. Monk helped the Redskins win three Super Bowls. When he left the team, Monk had 888 receptions. That is more than any other Redskin.

Darrell Green CORNERBACK (1983–2002)

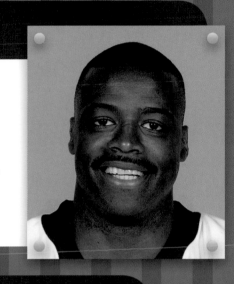

Darrell Green played for the Redskins his whole
career. He quickly became a star on the team's
defense. Green got an interception in 19 of his 20
seasons with the team. He had 54 interceptions in all.
That is more than any other Redskin. Green helped
the team make it to three Super Bowls and win two.

Robert Griffin III QUARTERBACK (2012–)

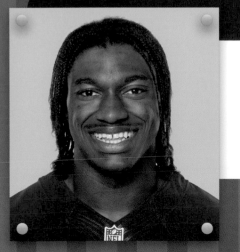

Robert Griffin III was the team's first choice in the
2012 draft. He was the second pick overall. Griffin
helped the Redskins make the play-offs his first
year. Griffin is often called "RG3."

FedExField

The Redskins play home games at FedExField. It is in Landover, Maryland, near Washington DC. FedExField opened in 1997. It can hold about 85,000 people.

Sean TAYLOR

FedExField has more regular seating than any other NFL stadium.

The Ring of Fame is on the upper deck of FedExField. It honors the team's greatest players, coaches, and businessmen.

23

Go Burgundy and Gold!

Thousands of fans flock to FedExField to see the Redskins play home games. They sing the team song, "Hail to the Redskins." Some fans call their team "the Burgundy and Gold."

In the 1980s, the team's powerful offensive line became known as "the Hogs." They got this nickname from offensive line coach Jim Bugel. Some fans continue to honor this fun nickname by wearing pig noses.

Final Call

The Redskins have a long, rich history. They won NFL championships as a young team. And, they won three Super Bowls in the 1980s and early 1990s.

Even during losing seasons, true fans have stuck by them. Many believe the Washington Redskins will remain one of the greatest teams in the NFL.

The Redskins are known for their faithful fans. They have sold out every home game since 1968! That is the longest streak in the NFL.

Through the Years

1932
The Boston Braves are founded by George Preston Marshall.

1933
The Boston Braves are renamed the Boston Redskins.

1942
The team wins a second NFL championship.

1936
The Redskins have their first winning season.

1937
Marshall moves the Redskins to Washington DC. Later that year, the team wins its first NFL **championship**.

1963

Sammy Baugh and George Preston Marshall become two of the first members of the Pro Football Hall of Fame.

1973

The Redskins play in their first Super Bowl.

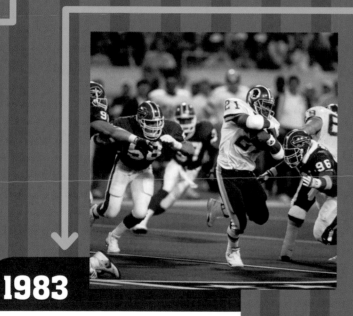

2012

The team chooses Robert Griffin III as the second overall pick in the **draft**. He helps the team make it to the play-offs during his first season.

1983

The Redskins get their first Super Bowl win. They beat the Miami Dolphins 27–17.

1992

The Redskins win their third Super Bowl.

Postgame Recap

1. Who was the coach of the Redskins during all three of their Super Bowl wins?

    A. George Allen   **B**. Joe Gibbs   **C**. George Preston Marshall

2. Where were the Redskins founded?

    A. Boston, Massachusetts
    B. Washington DC
    C. Baltimore, Maryland

3. Name 3 of the 19 Redskins in the Pro Football Hall of Fame.

4. How did Sammy Baugh help change the NFL?

    A. He helped make passing plays more popular.
    B. He invented the T-formation offense.
    C. He moved the team from Boston to the Washington DC.

Glossary

accurate free from mistakes.

career a period of time spent in a certain job.

champion the winner of a championship, which is a game, a match, or a race held to find a first-place winner.

draft a system for professional sports teams to choose new players. When a team drafts a player, they choose that player for their team.

interception (ihn-tuhr-SEHP-shuhn) when a player catches a pass that was meant for the other team's player.

retire to give up one's job.

rookie a first-year player in a professional sport.

Websites

To learn more about the NFL's Greatest Teams, visit **booklinks.abdopublishing.com**. These links are routinely monitored and updated to provide the most current information available.

Index